I Like Bugs

Angela Aylmore

Heinemann
LIBRARY

www.heinemann.co.uk/library
Visit our website to find out more information about Heinemann Library books.

To order:
 Phone 44 (0) 1865 888066
 Send a fax to 44 (0) 1865 314091
 Visit the Heinemann Bookshop at www.heinemann.co.uk/library to browse our catalogue and order online.

First published in Great Britain by Heinemann Library, Halley Court, Jordan Hill, Oxford OX2 8EJ, part of Harcourt Education. Heinemann is a registered trademark of Harcourt Education Ltd.

© Harcourt Education Ltd 2007
First published in paperback 2008
The moral right of the proprietor has been asserted.

Editorial: Dan Nunn and Sarah Chappelow
Design: Joanna Hinton-Malivoire
Picture research: Erica Newbery
Production: Duncan Gilbert

Origination: Chroma Graphics (Overseas) Pte. Ltd
Printed and bound in China, China by South China Printing Co. Ltd.

ISBN 978 0 431 10960 2 (hardback)
11 10 09 08 07
10 9 8 7 6 5 4 3 2 1

ISBN 978 0 431 10969 5 (paperback)
12 11 10 09 08
10 9 8 7 6 5 4 3 2 1

British Library Cataloguing in Publication Data
Aylmore, Angela
I like bugs. - (Things I like)
1. Insects - Juvenile literature
I. Title
595.7
A full catalogue record for this book is available from the British Library.

Acknowledgements
The publishers would like to thank the following for permission to reproduce photographs: Alamy p. 13 (Janine Wiedel Photolibrary); Ardea pp. 6 (Andy Teare), 12 (Steve Hopkin), 14–15 (Steve Hopkin), 20 (Pascal Goetgheluck); Corbis p. 7 (Anthony Bannister/Gallo Images); Digital Vision pp. 4–5 (green praying mantis); FLPA pp. 16 (Minden Pictures), 22 (ants, Minden Pictures); Getty images/Photodisc pp. 4–5 (caterpillar, butterfly, cricket, tarantula, bee, praying mantis), 10 (all photos), 22 (beetle); Nature Picture Library pp. 9 (Tom Vezo), 11 (Kim Taylor), 17 (Phil Savoie), 22 (centipede, Tom Vezo), 18 (Wegner/ARCO), 19 (Wegner/ARCO), 22 (tarantula, Wegner/ARCO); NHPA pp. 8, 21. Cover photograph of a spider reproduced with permission of Corbis (Joe MacDonald).

Contents

Some words are shown in bold, like this. You can find out what they mean by looking in the Glossary.

Bugs

I like bugs.

I will tell you my favourite things about bugs.

Centipedes

My favourite bug is the centipede. Centipedes have lots of legs.

Centipedes live in **damp** places.

Centipedes can be many colours. This one has a brown body and yellow legs!

This kind of centipede is the biggest in the world. It lives in **Trinidad**.

Beetles

I like lots of different types of beetle.

Beetles have two sets of wings.
One set is hard. One set is soft.

hard wings

soft wings

Ladybirds are a type of beetle. I see lots of ladybirds in my garden.

This is a Hercules beetle. It is the largest beetle in the world!

Ants

I like to watch ants. I have seen them outside and at the zoo. Ants make lots of tunnels.

queen ant

This is the queen ant.
She lays all the eggs.

These are the worker ants.
They take care of the
queen and her eggs.

Giant spiders

This is my pet tarantula.

Tarantulas are spiders.
They have eight legs.

I feed my spider crickets.
In the wild she would
catch her own food.

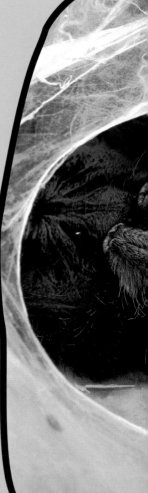

My spider has oily feet. They stop her sticking to her **web**.

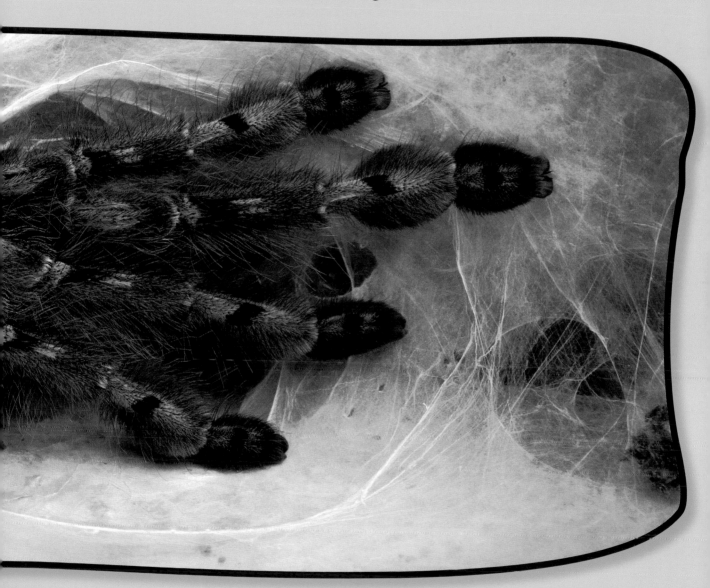

Do you like bugs?

Now you know why I like bugs! Do you like bugs too?

Glossary

damp slightly wet

Trinidad an island in the Caribbean Sea

web fine threads spun by a spider to
catch flies

Find out more

Usborne Spotter's Guide: Bugs and Insects (Usborne Publishing Limited, 2006)

Find out about lots of different bugs at this website: www.pestworldforkids.org/

Index